THIS IS A CARLTON BOOK.

This edition published by Carlton Books Limited 1994.

© 1994 Holoquest. All rights reserved.

ISBN 1-85868-063-8

Printed and bound in Italy.

3D ART

EXPERIENCE

THE AMAZING

IMAGES

CAUSING A

GLOBAL

SENSATION

CARLTON

Welcome to the

The images that you are about to see have an amazing history dating back over 100 years. They are the latest products of a medium that has been in development since Sir Charles Wheatstone invented the stereo viewer in 1838 — a year before the photographic camera!

Despite what cynics might say, 3D Art is far from faddish (even the great surrealist painter, Salvador Dali, made use of what was called Stereography).

But the images in 3D Art are different, they need no complex viewing equipment, nor do they need any special appreciation of 'Art' (with a capital 'A').

Computers have made it easier to produce the stereo effects and the sumptuous colours and patterns that make the images in 3D Art leap out at you. But it is still the imaginations and skills of the artists that make it all worth while.

So now, using this book, and nothing more than your own eyes and little patience, you too can enter a whole new dimension of visual thrills.

Don't worry if at first you can't make out the individually crafted, three-dimensional images specially commissioned for 3D Art. This is a common problem and has little to do with your eyesight. In actual fact, it has more to do with your state of mind and ability to relax.

To discover whether or not you can see stereo-3D Art, try this easy test. Get a pencil or pen and hold it up at arm's length.

Now, stare through it (try focusing on what's behind it, a door for example).

world of 3D Art

After a few seconds you should be able to see two pens — remember, don't look at them, look through them.

Passed the test? Most people will have done, now it's time for the next step in your sensational journey...

Take a deep breath, forget all your everyday cares and turn to whichever splash of colour on whichever page appeals to you most — it makes no difference which image you decide to look at first, the choice is entirely yours.

Remember not to look at the patterns that overlay the images. Try to look through them. Here's an exercise that works for many, many people:

Bring the book close to your face, so that it nearly touches your nose. Unless you've got superhuman sight, this should take the 3D Art out of focus. Relax, don't try to make out an image. Try to stare through it.

Once your eyes have accustomed themselves to the new focus, very slowly move the book away. Remember don't focus on the page.

As you move the book away the image hidden within should come into focus and you'll be rewarded with a three-dimensional picture coming out of the page towards you.

Don't worry if you can't make out the image, or if your brain makes your eyes focus on the page. Viewing 3D Art can take some practice.

Now all you have to do is marvel at the stunning 3D Art. You might even find it helping you to relax too.

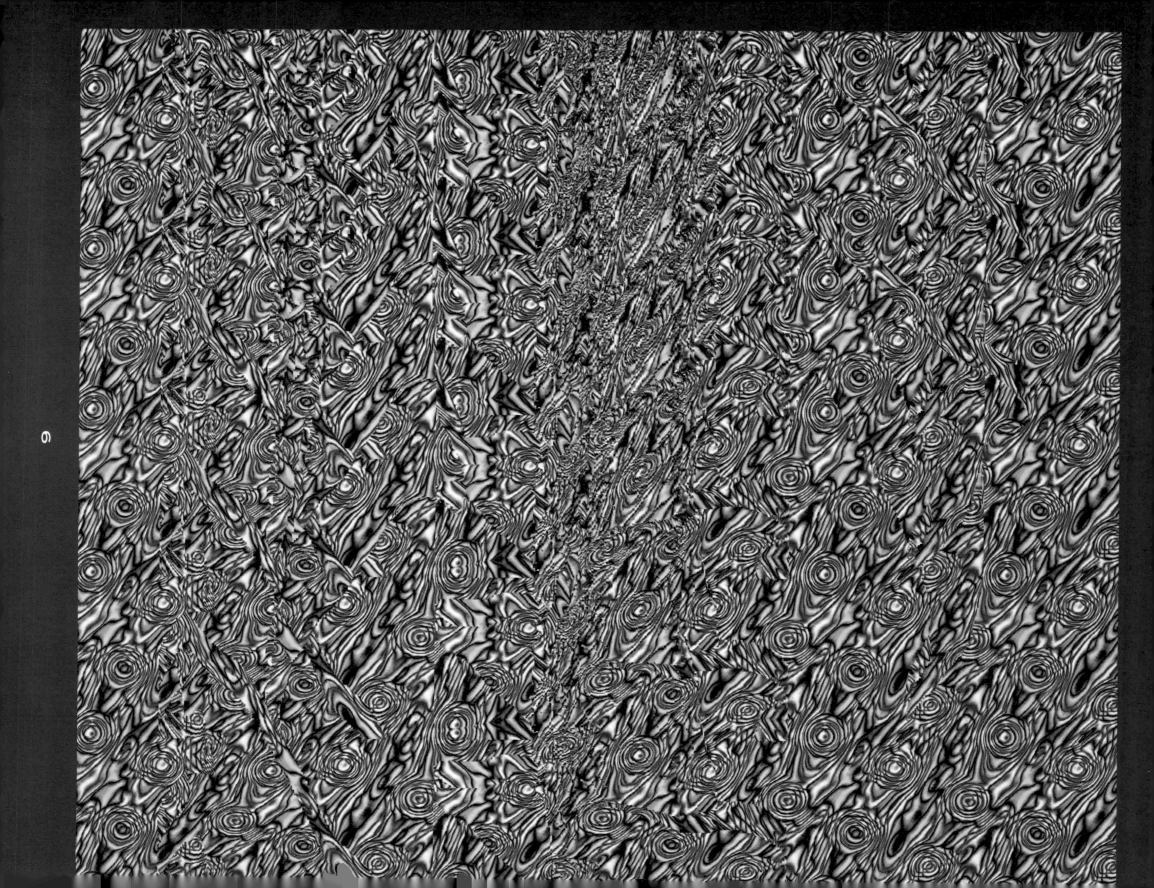

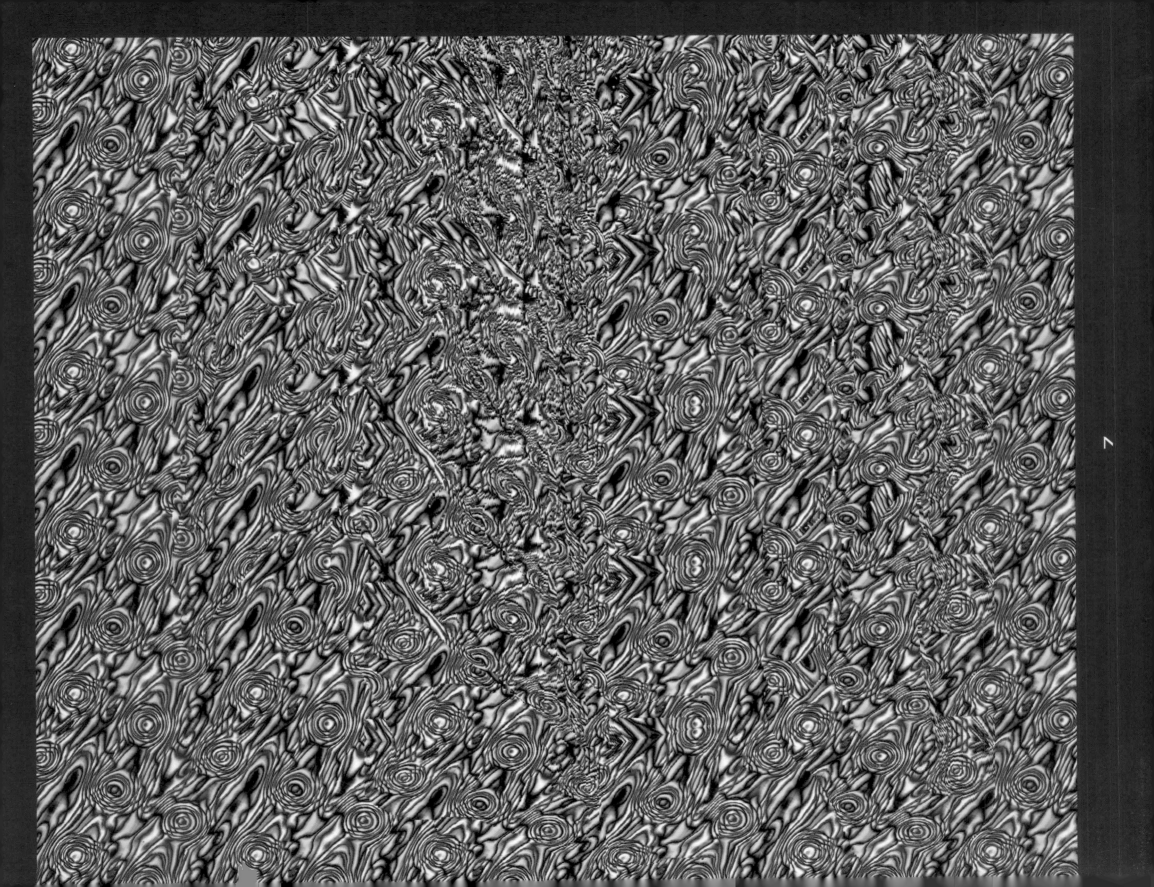

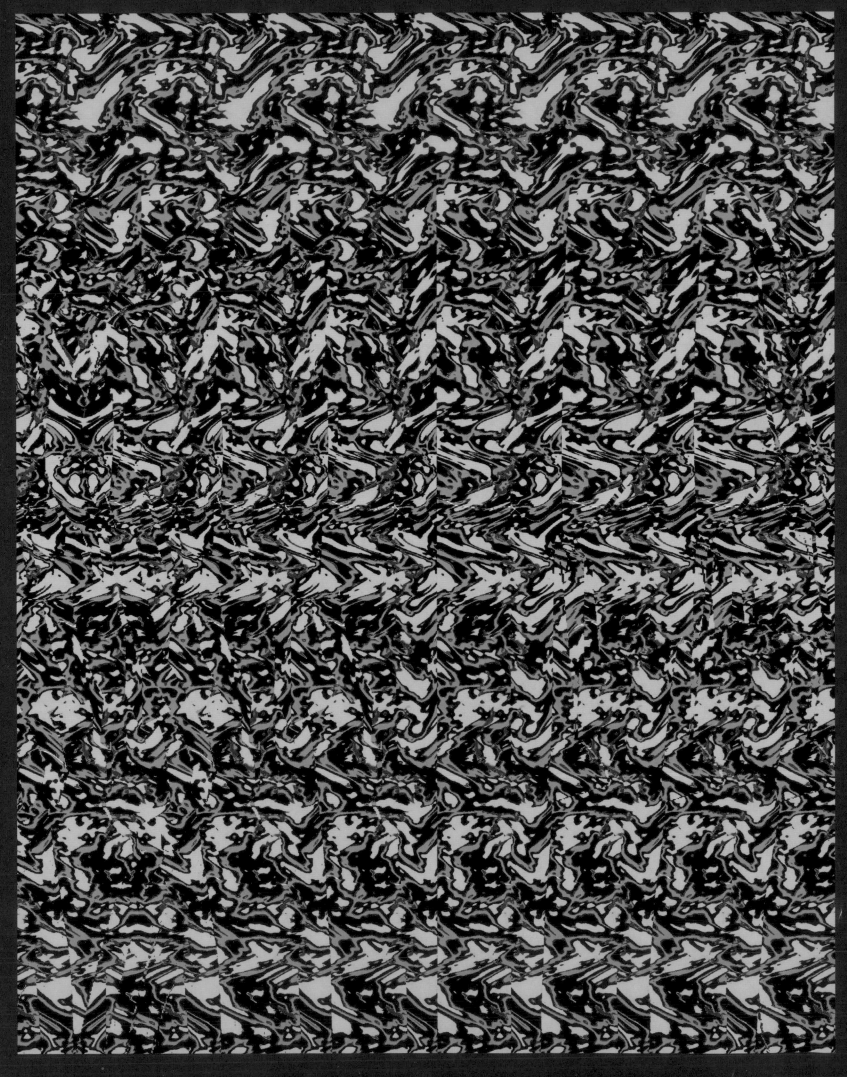

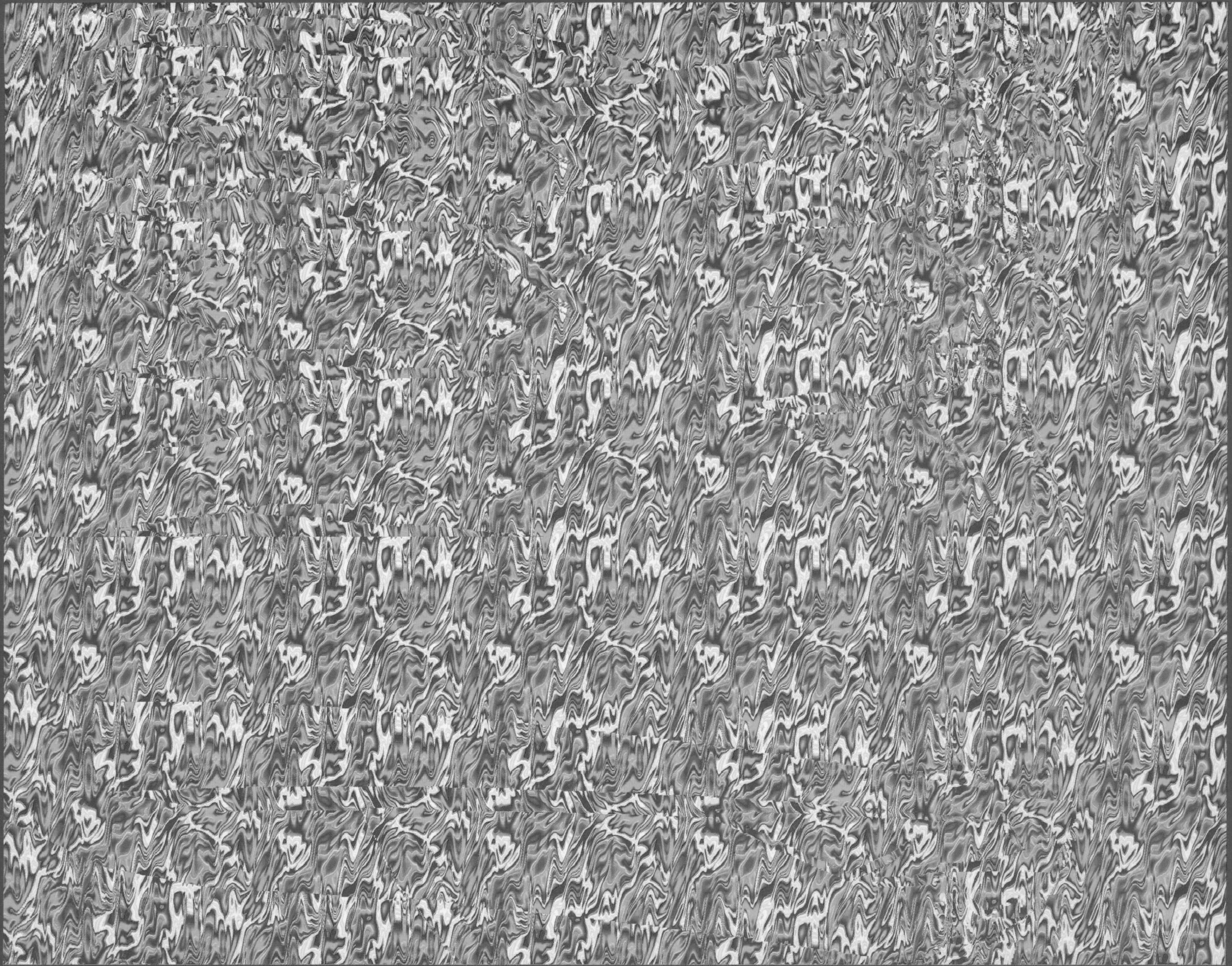

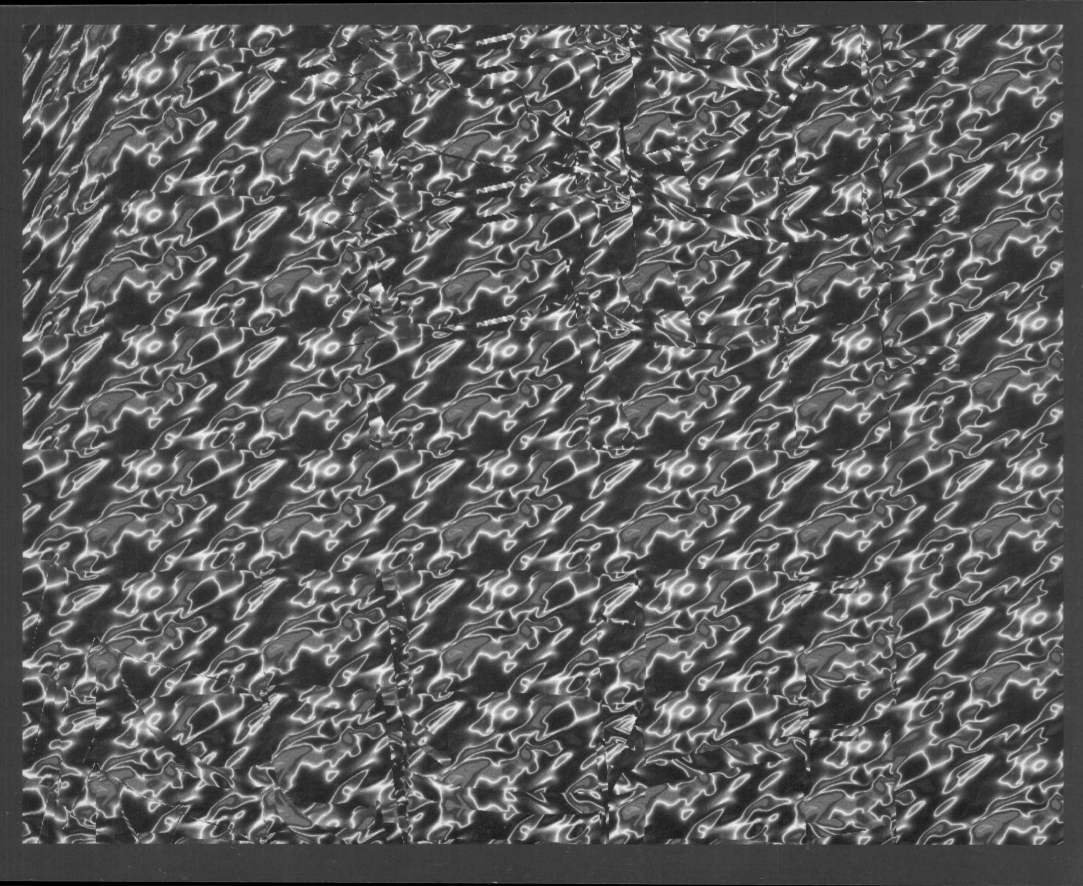

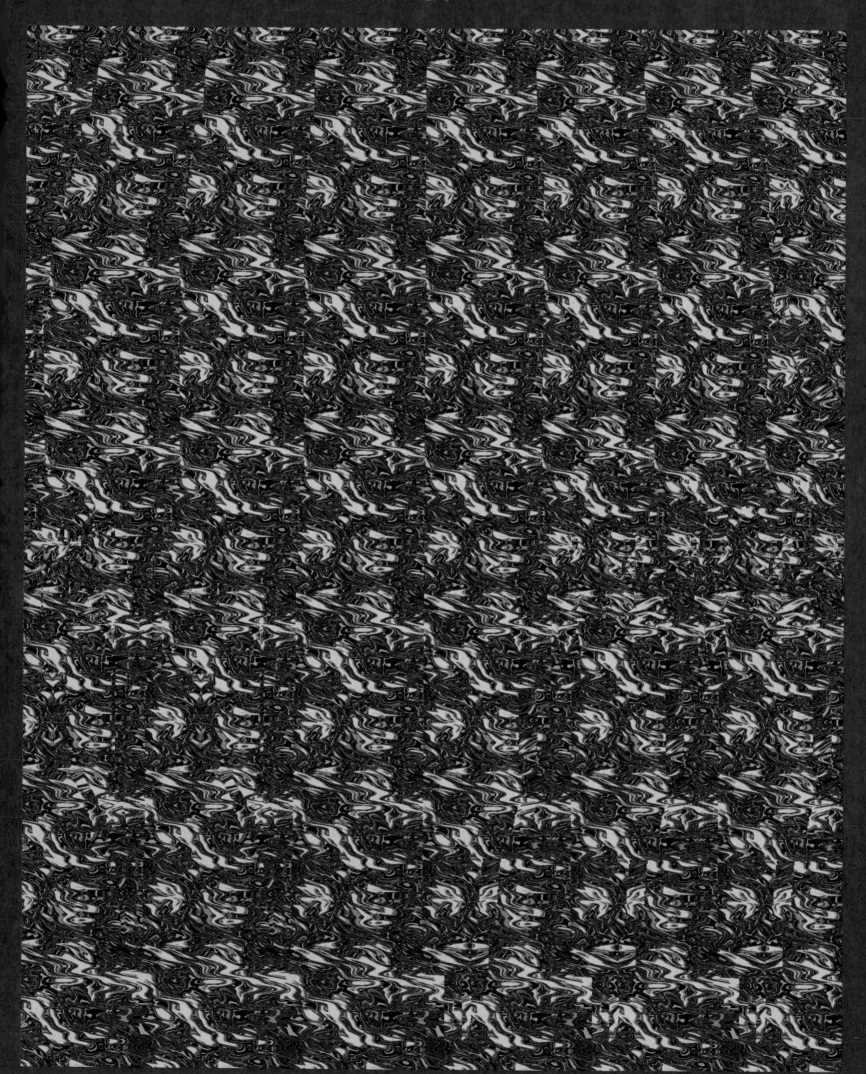

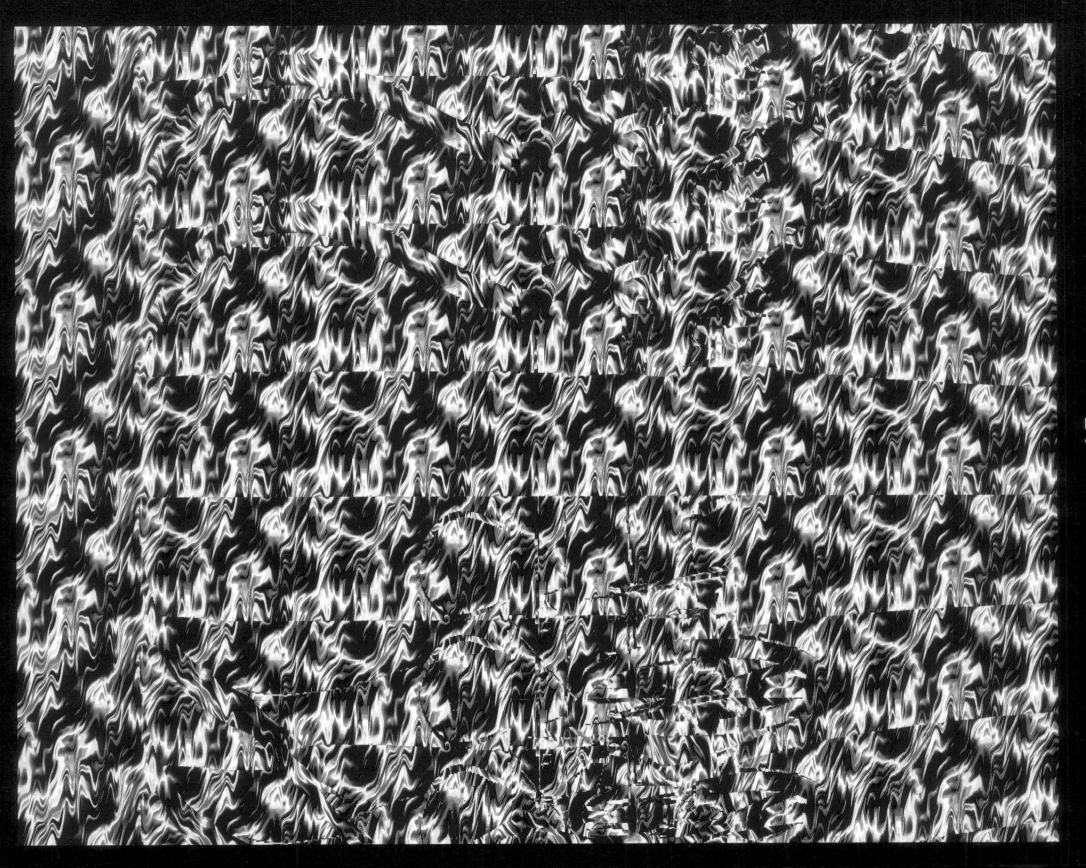

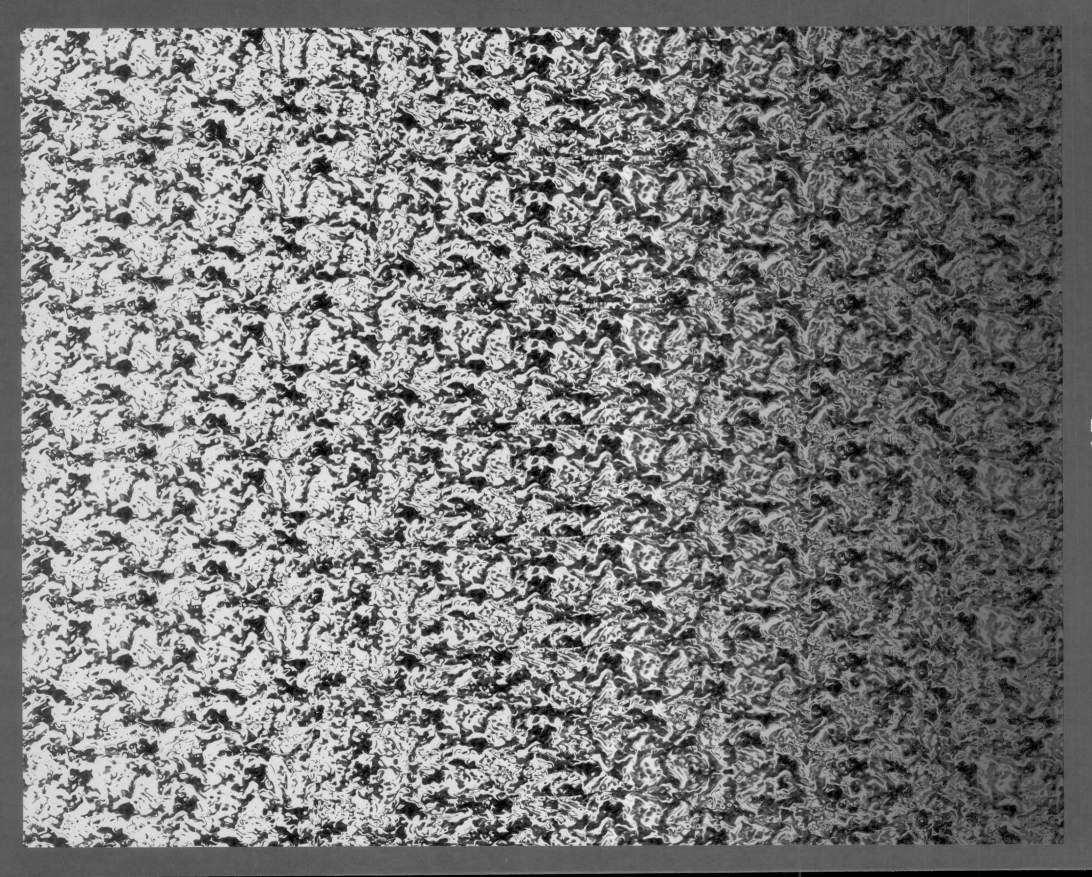

17

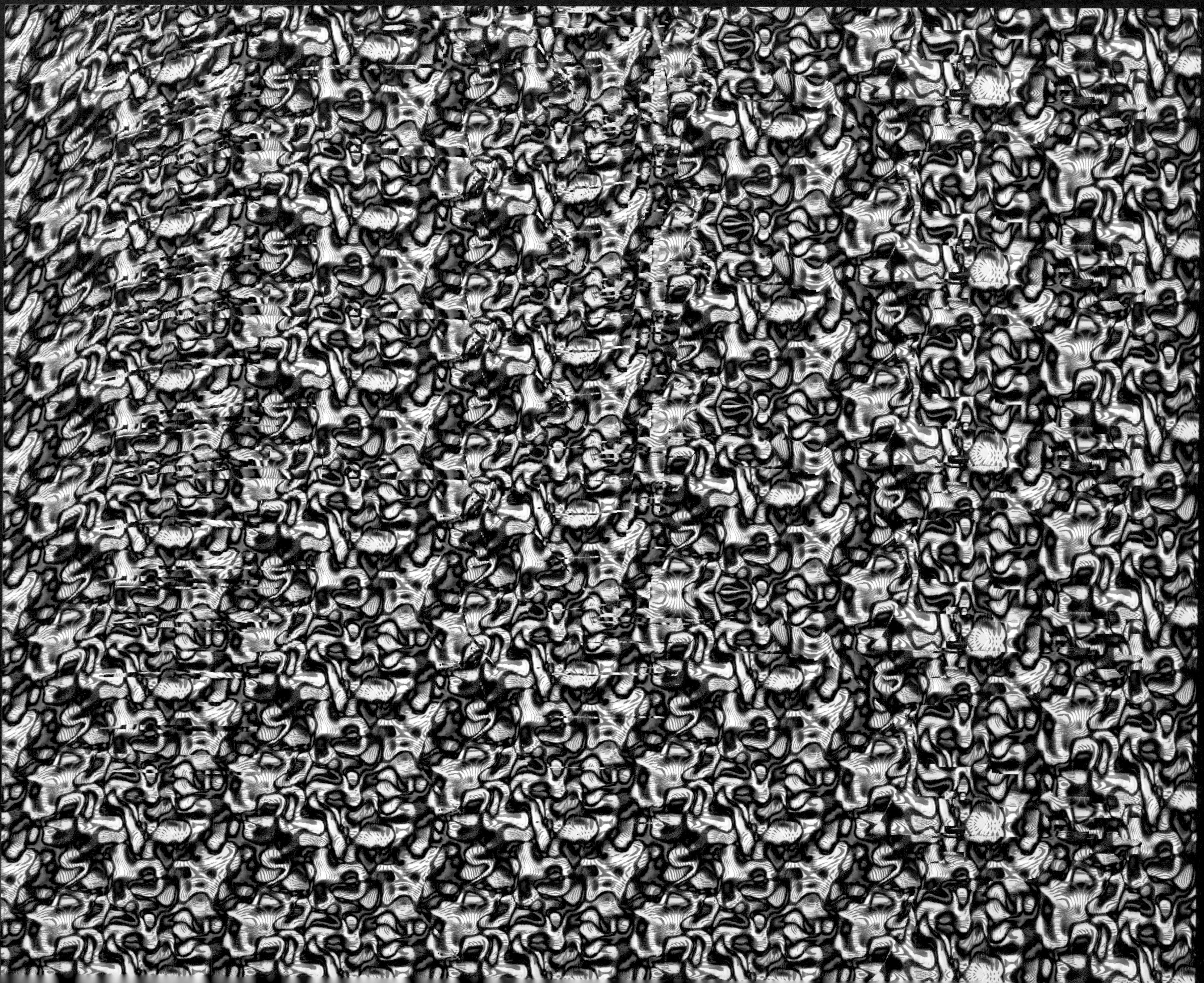

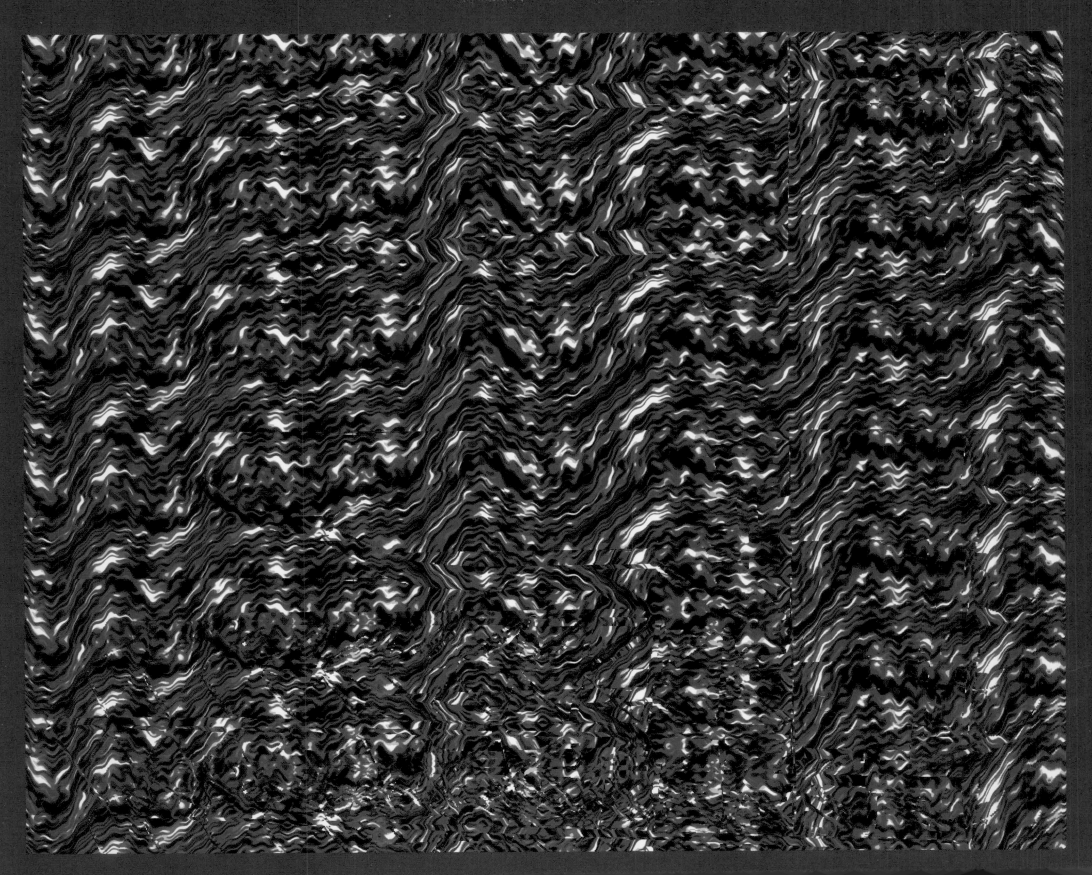

21

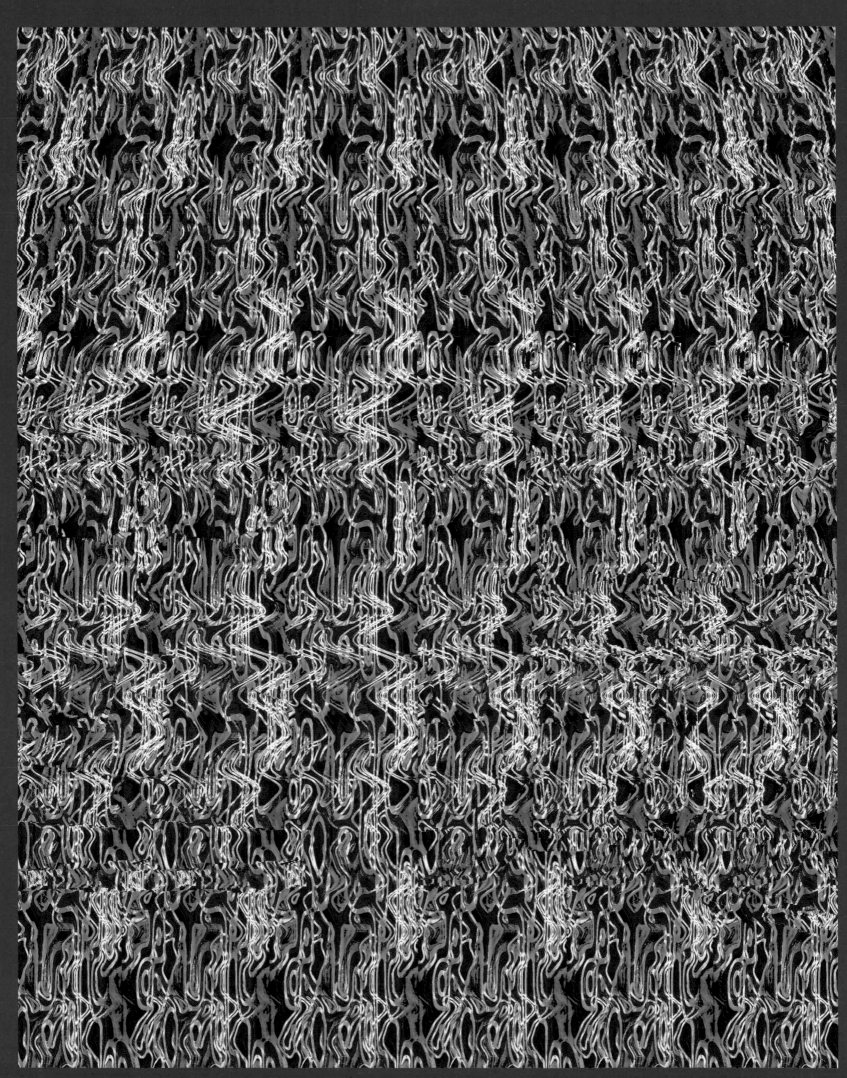

23

24

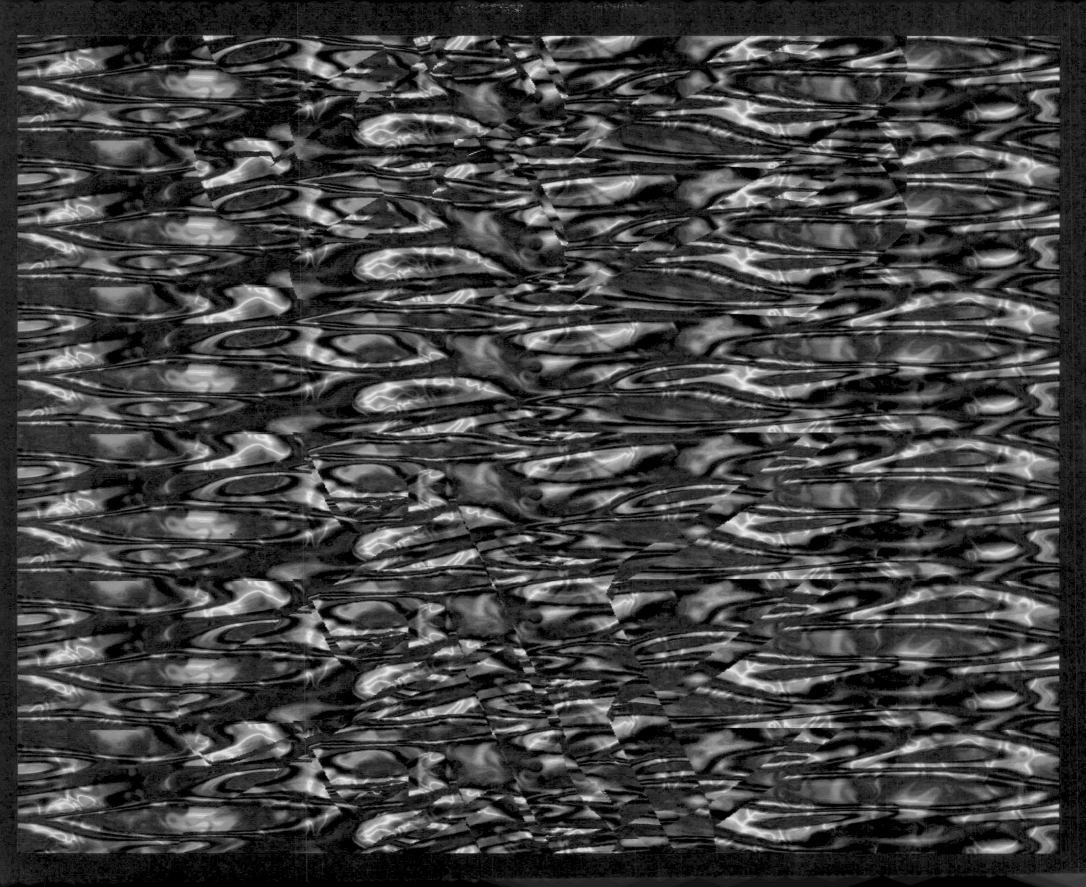

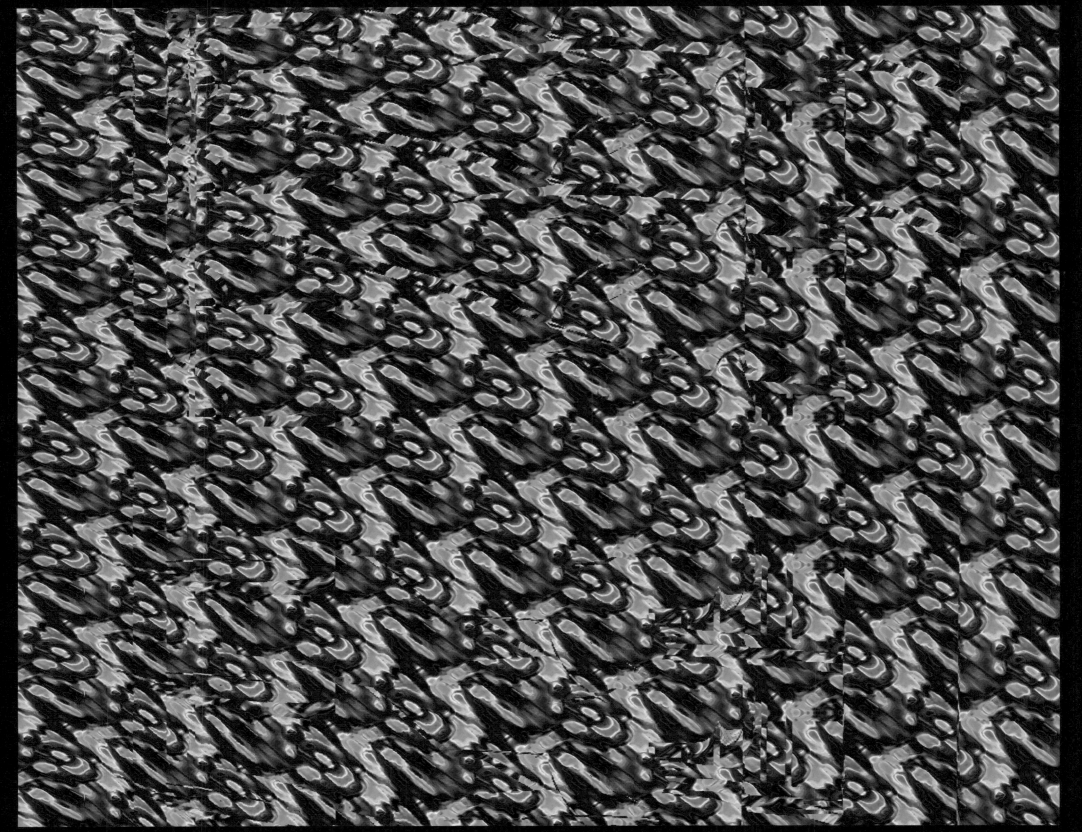

28

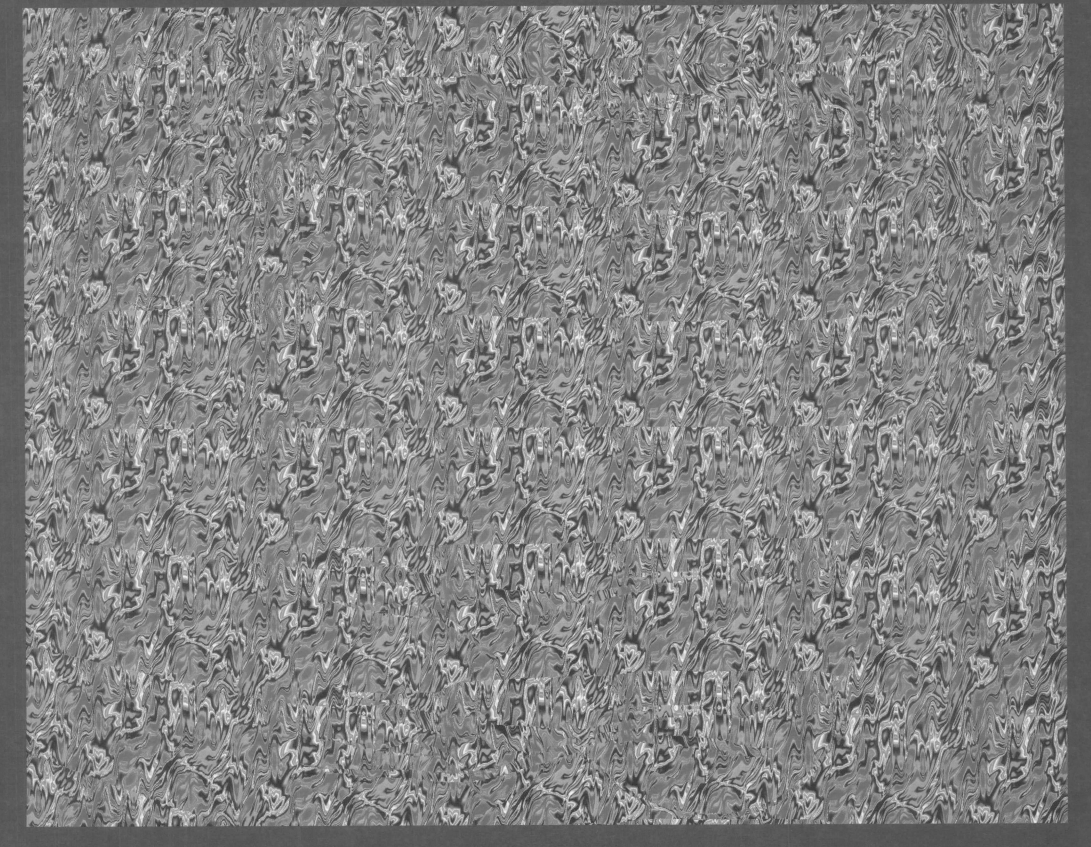

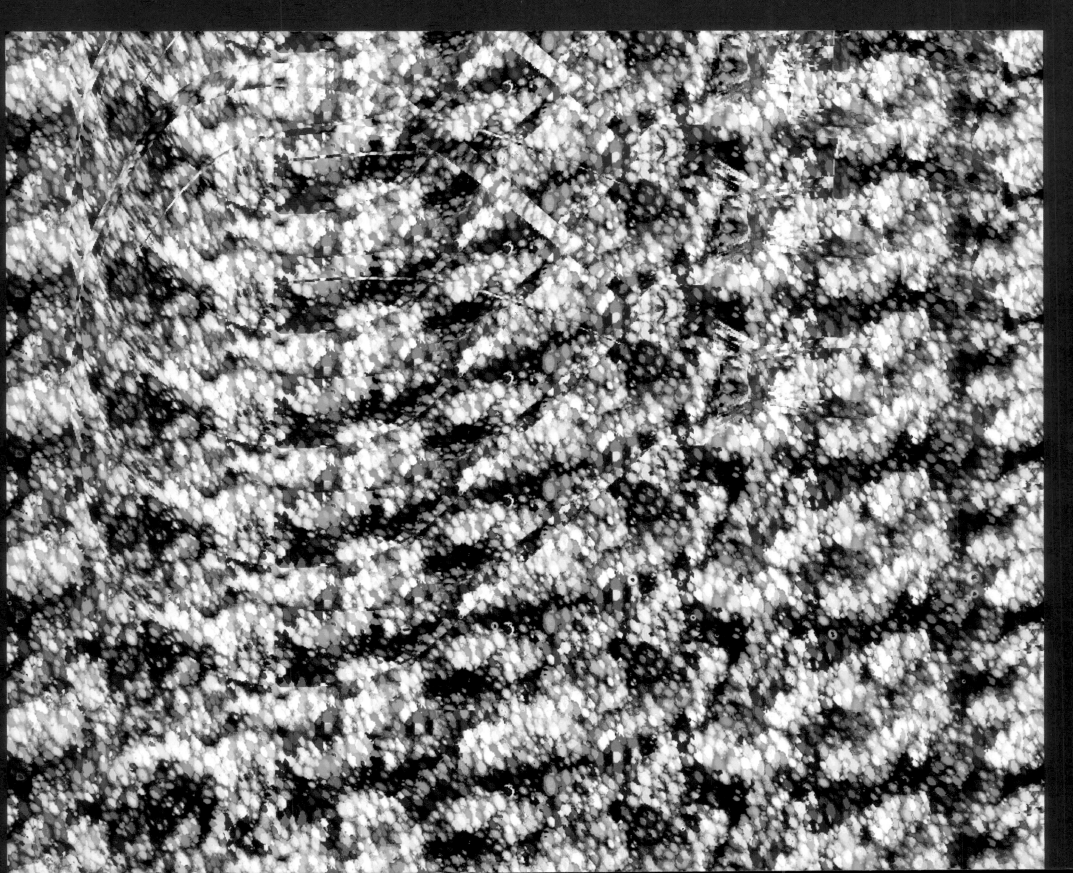

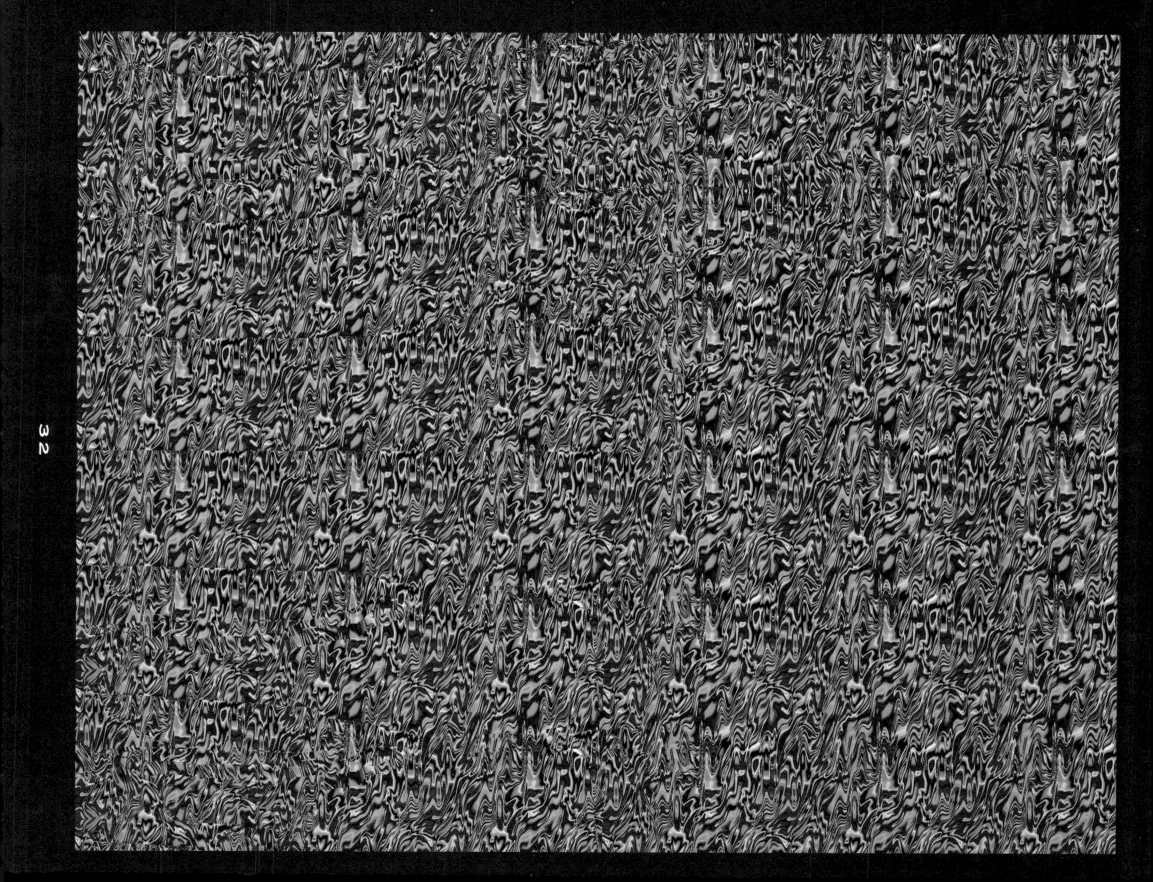

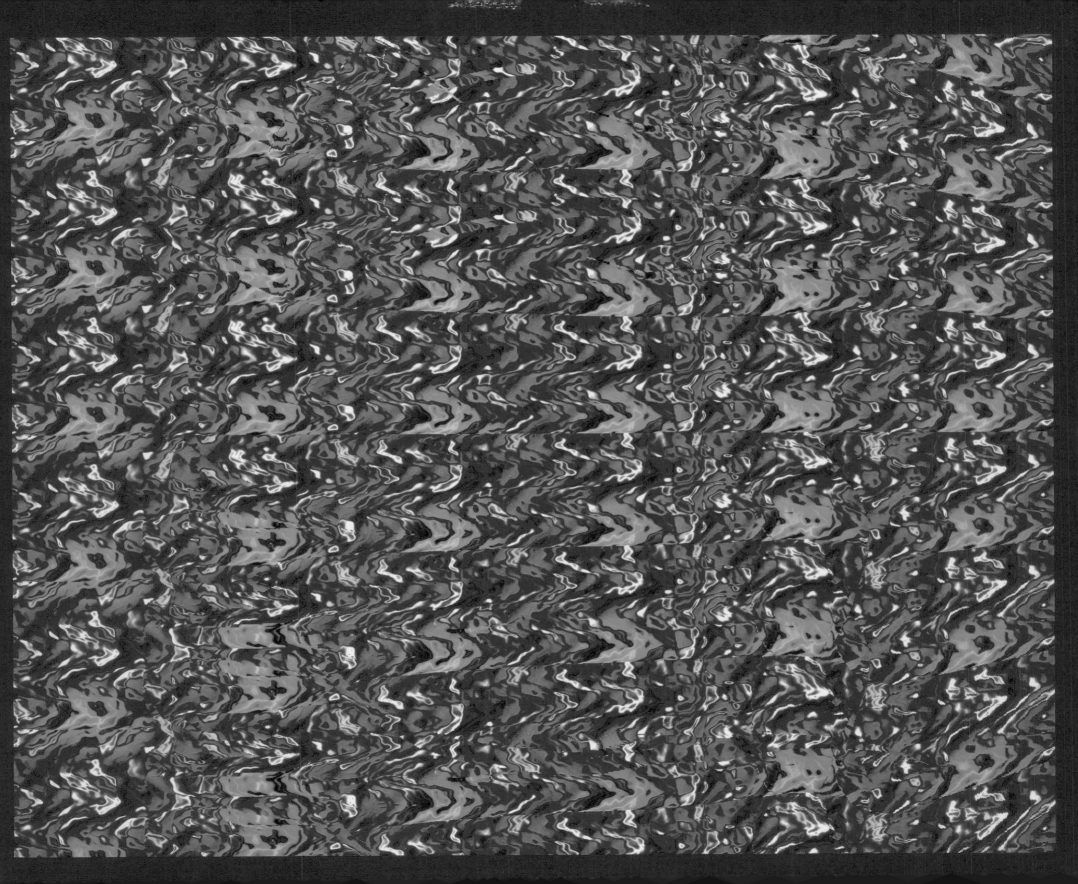

33

34

35

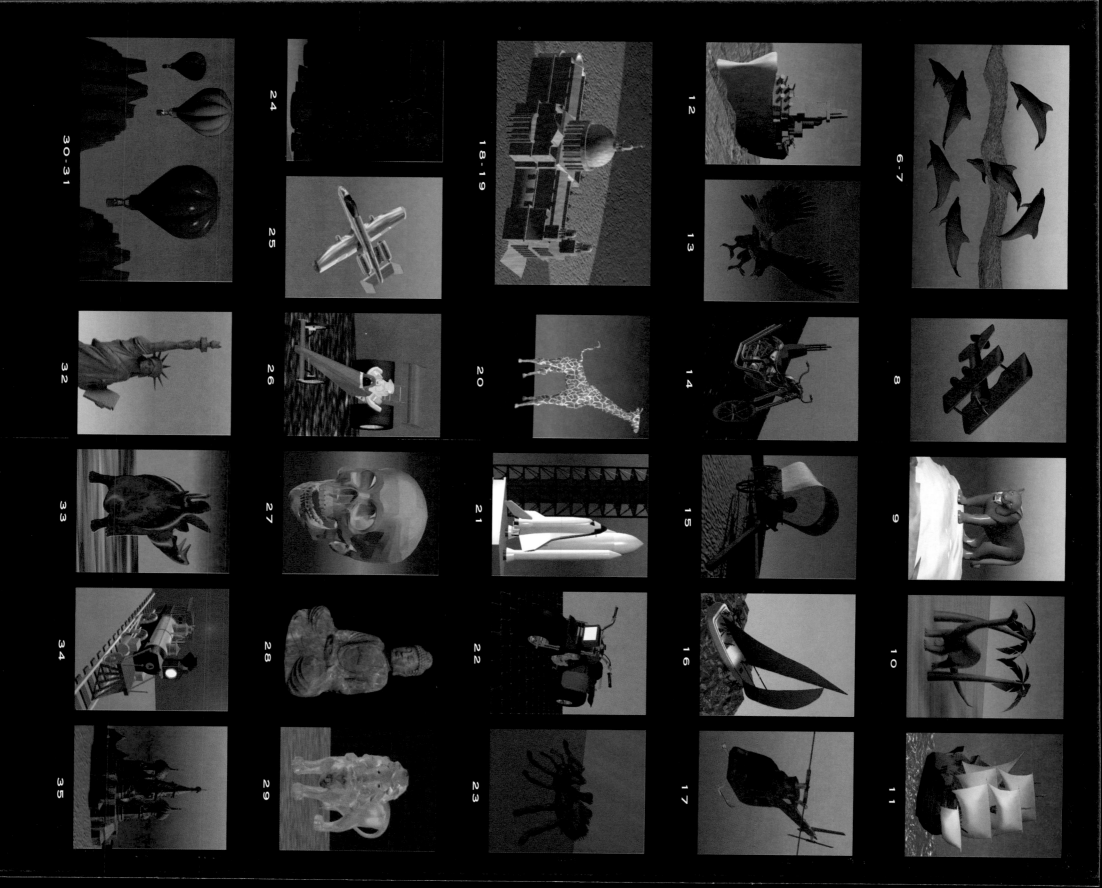